# DK SUPERGUIDES
# SNOWBOARDING

Neutral stance

Traversing

Warming up

Gliding forward

Getting up toeside

Landing safely

# DK SUPERGUIDES

# SNOWBOARDING

Written by Steve Davis
Foreword by Bryan Iguchi

Gearing up

Getting to your feet

Racing

Falling backward

Running flat

DK

A DORLING KINDERSLEY BOOK

# Dorling DK Kindersley

LONDON, NEW YORK, SYDNEY, DELHI, PARIS,
MUNICH and JOHANNESBURG

**Project Editor** Stella Love, Lee Simmons
**Art Editor** Lesley Betts, Tassy King
**Designer** Sarah Cowley
**DTP Designer** Almudena Díaz
**Photography** James Jackson
**Picture Research** Neil Armstrong, Frankie Marking
**Production** Josie Alabaster, Orla Creegan
**US Editor** Kristin Ward

### The young snowboarders
Tariq Alatas, Kate Blackshaw, Rachel Davis, Ryan Davis, Arash Hamrahian

Published in the United States by
Dorling Kindersley Publishing, Inc
95 Madison Avenue, New York, New York 10016

First published as *The Young Snowboarder*, 1997
First American Edition, 1997
Revised American Edition, 2000
2 4 6 8 10 9 7 5 3

Copyright © 1997, 2000 Dorling Kindersley Limited, London

Dorling Kindersley books are available at special discounts for bulk purchases for sales promotions or premiums. Special editions, including personalized covers, excerpts of existing guides, and corporate imprints can be created in large quantities for specific needs. For more information, contact Special Markets Dept./Dorling Kindersley Publishing, Inc./95 Madison Ave,/New York, NY 10016/Fax: 800-600-9098.

ISBN 0-7894-6541-8

Color reproduction by Colourscan, Singapore
Printed and bound in Italy by L.E.G.O.

see our complete
catalog at
**www.dk.com**

# Contents

*"My goal is to ride as much powder as possible, but I also enjoy surfing and skateboarding."*

# To all young snowboarders

THE MOUNTAINS OFFER a special kind of peace and freedom that you just don't find anywhere else. I, like many people, have discovered that snowboarding is more than just a sport, it is a lifestyle. Dedication and patience will lead to fun days of riding with friends. Snowboarding has also taught me to respect nature and appreciate the benefits of being athletic. Through competition, I've learned to deal with fears and remain calm in tough situations. I hope snowboarding will bring as much excitement into your life as it has into mine.

*Bryan Iguchi*

*"Riding fresh powder snow is the essence of snowboarding."*

*"Many snowboarding tricks were first done on skateboards, like the one I am doing here. It's called a method air."*

*"Jumping cliffs can be fun, as long as you make sure your landing is safe! But be careful – this sort of trick is only for very experienced riders. Don't try it yourself."*

# History of snowboarding

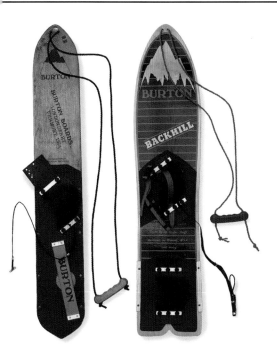

SNOWBOARDING BEGAN in the US in the 1960s when Sherman Poppen invented the "snurfer" – a simple board with a rope handle attached to its nose. Snurfing as a sport was taken up by a number of surf, ski, and skateboard enthusiasts who then started to improve on the idea. Jake Burton Carpenter attached rubber foot straps to boards and a former skateboard world champion, Tom Sims, also started developing new boards, experimenting with different shapes and materials. By the late 1970s, snowboarding, as it came to be called, was well on its way to becoming an established sport.

## Early boards
One of the biggest breakthroughs in the design of early boards was made when an American, Jake Burton Carpenter, had the idea of attaching adjustable foot straps. These early bindings had a major impact on the development of the sport since they gave the rider much more control over the board and allowed longer descents to be made.

## Pioneers
Like Jake Burton Carpenter, Tom Sims was one of the pioneers of snowboarding, both in the development of boards and as a rider. In 1981, on a steel-edged board, he won the slalom title of the first snowboard championships, which were held in the US. (Slalom is riding downhill on a wavy course marked with flags.)

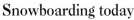

## Snowboarding today
Today, with media coverage of events and readily available equipment, snowboarding has become very popular. Some people are attracted by the excitement of aerial tricks or racing while others are simply eager to try their slope skills. In either case, more enthusiasts are taking up snowboarding each year.

## Freeriding fun
Freeriding is the most widespread form of snowboarding. Once you have learned the basic techniques of boarding, a mountain is yours to explore, with a choice of runs to follow, or naturally formed bumps, jumps, and gullies to ride.

## Modern racing
Racing is the speed discipline of snowboarding. A combination of skill, courage, and advances in equipment technology allows today's racers to carve their turns through the slalom gates at amazing speeds.

## Freestyle
Freestyle riding incorporates all the gravity-defying tricks and spins. This style of snowboarding can be fiercely competitive, with new and daring tricks being invented all the time.

# Getting ready

SNOWBOARDING is an exciting sport, but, whether you plan to ride on artificial slopes or in the mountains, it is important to be properly equipped and to follow some basic safety advice. A good sporting goods store will help you choose boots, boards, and bindings, and also clothing that is practical and appropriate for your style of snowboarding.

## What to wear

In the mountains, be prepared for changeable and extreme weather. You will need a weatherproof jacket and pants. Wear layers of warm clothing, rather than one thick item. You can always take a layer off if you get too warm. Sunglasses or goggles are vital to protect your eyes from bright sunlight reflecting off the snow.

*The leash is a safety strap to attach the board to your leg to stop it from sliding away from you. The leash should be the first thing you put on when you reach the slopes and the last thing you take off when you leave!*

## Top safety tips

1. When entering a slope or starting downhill, stop and observe all other users first.
2. Always behave in a way that does not endanger or prejudice others.
3. Adapt your speed to suit your ability.
4. A person coming from above must avoid colliding with others downhill of them.
5. Leave plenty of space when overtaking.
6. Exercise caution and look around when turning on your heelside, to avoid blindspots.
7. Always wear a leash attached to your front leg.
8. If you fall, move to the side as soon as possible. Only stop where you can easily be seen.
9. When climbing up or down, keep to the side of the slope.
10. Obey all signs and markings.
11. Only use authorized areas.

*You will need sunglasses or goggles with tinted lenses to protect your eyes. There are also specific tints to help you see dips and bumps in the snow on dull days.*

*Sunscreen should always be used to protect you from sunburn and chapping in cold winds. A lip balm will prevent your lips from cracking.*

## Equipment

It's a good idea to rent equipment when you first go snowboarding, until you know what you like, and what is right for you.

*A freeride board is fairly wide and flexible. Racing boards are stiff and narrow by comparison.*

## Pants

Your pants need to be comfortable and loose-fitting. Look for a pair with extra padding around the knees and bottom to protect you when you fall!

*A backpack is a good way to carry things such as spare clothing, snacks, and a tool kit.*

*On cold days, you will need a warm hat that covers your ears. Some jackets have a useful hood tucked into the collar.*

**Safety first**
Helmets can provide extra protection from falls and collisions. Ask your local supplier for details.

## Jacket

Snowboarding jackets are expensive, but you can wear them all through the winter. Look for one that is loose-fitting, comfortable, long enough at the back to cover your bottom, and high enough at the neck to keep out the wind and cold.

*Gloves are essential to protect your hands on dryslopes and in the snow. Some have a strap to protect your wrists from injury and a drawstring to keep the snow out.*

## Tool kit

It is useful to carry a small wrench and a screwdriver to adjust your bindings, and rub-on wax for your board. Wax helps the board run well. There are different types of wax for different snow conditions.

*Board waxes*

*Multihead screwdriver*

*½-in (10-mm) wrench*

*Soft boots are very popular because they are comfortable and flexible.*

# Boots and bindings

Boots and bindings are designed to work together as a "system." There are three main types:

## Step-in system

This is the newest system. The boot has a built-in metal bail screwed to its base that clicks into a spring-loaded binding as you step onto the board.

*Release lever*

*Metal bail*

*Lace-up, step-in boot*

## Soft-boot system

This is the system most people start with. It is also preferred for freestyle riding. The binding has a calf support at the back and straps to lock your foot in place.

*Toe strap*

*Standard lace-up soft boot*

## Hard-boot system

This system is best for high-speed turns and racing. The metal bails of the binding snap down on the toe and heel ridge of the hard plastic outer shell of the boots.

*Heel bail*    *Toe bail*    *Clip fastener*

*Hard boot with ratcheted fastenings*

# Board talk

Which leg do you favor? If you prefer to lead with your left foot forward, you are a regular rider. If you prefer your right foot in front, you are riding goofy!

Most boards are similar in shape to the one below – wide at the nose and tail, but narrowing at the waist. Race boards are longer and narrower, while freestyle boards are shorter and wider.

*Regular*    *Goofy*

*Tail*    *Waist*    *Nose*

# Starting out

THE FIRST FEW TIMES you clip on the bindings of your snowboard, it will probably feel strange. But you will soon develop a routine of checking your board and bindings, fastening the safety leash, and clipping your front foot in first. On this page you will discover some basic ways of maneuvering on your board with just your front foot clipped in. These are basic skills, but you will find that they often come in handy.

# Getting on the board

Put your board across the slope and kneel on your back leg, facing uphill. Clip on the safety leash so that the board cannot slide away.

**1** Clip the leash around your front leg and put that foot into its binding.

**2** Push your heel well back into the binding and fasten the ankle strap.

**3** Now fasten the toe strap. Then stand up and use the toe edge as a brake.

## Step, skate, and turn

Moving on flat ground is something you need to learn how to do. Here is a sequence of basic skills for you to try so that you can move easily on the level.

*Stomp pad*

**Stomp pad**
This is a nonslip pad next to the rear binding on which you can rest your free foot when skating.

*Turn your shoulders and upper body to face the direction of travel.*

*Don't look down to locate the stomp pad.*

**1** Start by walking the board along, taking small steps. Place your free foot close to the toes of your front foot for each step.

**2** Then try skating along. Push from your free foot to make the board glide forward. Keep the board flat.

*Safety leash*

**3** Try to hold the gliding position longer each time you skate, and rest your free foot on the stomp pad.

# Walking on the level

There will always be times when you need to unclip your back foot and take a few steps.

*Drive your arms to help you move along.*

*Keep each step fairly small.*

*Slide the board along with your front foot.*

**1** Release your back foot from its binding and take a step with it parallel to your board.

**2** Push with your free foot to slide the board forward. Use the swing of your arms to help.

# Walking uphill

Sometimes you will need to take a few steps up a slope, in a ski-lift line, for example.

*Keep your board horizontal across the slope.*

*Dig the toe edge in to stop the board from sliding away from you.*

**1** Release your back foot and step uphill onto it, turning your board across the slope.

**2** Lift the board up, digging the toe edge into the slope before you take the next step.

**4** To turn the board to face a new direction, take a small step away from its toe edge onto your free foot.

**5** Tilt the board onto its toe edge behind you. Then lift or drag it to bring the nose around to your free foot.

**6** Take another step into the turn and lift the board around again. Keep your steps small and your feet fairly close together.

*On icy ground, turn in lots of small stages.*

*Take small steps with your free foot.*

*The toe edge of the board will give you stability, so use it to help you.*

*Nose*

15

# Falling safely

NO MATTER HOW good you get at snowboarding, there are going to be times when you fall over. Learning how to fall will help prevent injuries to your hands and wrists, and make those falls less jarring. Also, knowing how to get back onto your feet from your toe edge will save you a lot of fatigue and frustration, particularly during your early lessons.

## Falling backward

If you catch a heel edge and fall backward, try to relax, crouch, and roll.

*Don't put your hands down.*

**1** Tuck in your elbows and hold your hands close to your chest.

*As you start to fall, quickly get as low as you can.*

*Tuck in your chin.*

**2** Crouch to get your bottom close to your heel edge.

**3** Round your spine and let yourself roll back

*Roll to absorb the impact.*

## Falling forward

The important thing when falling is to keep your arms tucked in until you're on the ground. Then use your forearms to protect your head from the ground.

**2** Drop onto your knees as you fall forward, then use your forearms to cushion the landing.

*Tuck in your elbows.*

*Use your forearms, not your hands.*

**1** Clench your fists and tuck in your elbows. Hold your arms close to your chest.

*You can wear extra padding on your knees.*

**3** Get back onto your feet by walking your hands back toward the board.

*Dig your toe edge in as you get back up.*

## Getting up toeside

It is easier to get up on your toe edge than your heel edge, so if you fall backward, roll the board over like this.

*Start to take this hand over and reach out in front of you.*

*Lift with your front leg, keeping the tail still.*

*Angle the board with your legs.*

*Tail*

**1** Sit back, resting on your hands. Keep your board tail still and use your front leg to pull the nose in toward you.

*Support yourself on your hands.*

**2** Roll onto your side and start to lift the nose of your board. Keep the tail in the same spot on the ground.

## Basic stances

There are two basic stances, or positions, you will use on your board time and time again. Both should feel natural and comfortable.

### Riding stance

This is the position for going straight along or down the hill with the base of your board flat.

*Keep your forearms lifted.*

*Keep your back straight.*

*Turn squarely onto your toe edge.*

### Neutral stance

This is the position to use, with your weight evenly divided over both feet, for braking or sideslipping – in other words, when using your edges to skid to a stop.

# Basic riding position

Here you can see a basic riding position. Everyone will vary this position slightly to suit their own style of riding, but the principles remain the same. Basic posture is for moving forward, so you need to look where you are going and guide your board.

*Look in the direction in which you are traveling.*

*Rotate your upper body slightly toward the nose of your board.*

*Aim your leading hand along the path you want to take.*

*Try to keep your back leg relaxed.*

*Flex your front knee so it can act as a shock absorber.*

*Take your weight slightly forward, onto your front foot.*

*Keep your board running flat on the ground.*

*Nose*

*This position should feel relaxed and comfortable.*

*Tail*

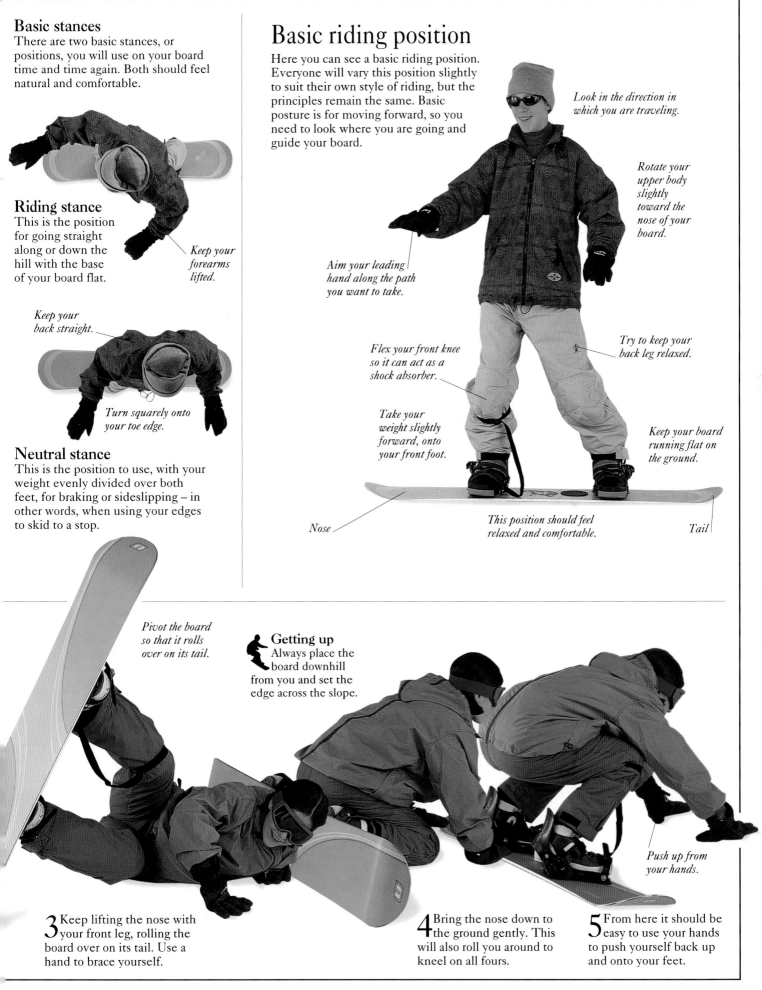

*Pivot the board so that it rolls over on its tail.*

**Getting up**
Always place the board downhill from you and set the edge across the slope.

*Push up from your hands.*

**3** Keep lifting the nose with your front leg, rolling the board over on its tail. Use a hand to brace yourself.

**4** Bring the nose down to the ground gently. This will also roll you around to kneel on all fours.

**5** From here it should be easy to use your hands to push yourself back up and onto your feet.

# Warming up

**B**EFORE YOU SET OFF, it is essential to wake up your body by warming and stretching your muscles. Working through some warm-up exercises will increase your heartbeat and breathing rate, and loosen your muscles and joints. This will help you avoid injury when snowboarding. It will also give you a chance to give your equipment a final check and make sure your boots and bindings are firmly fastened and comfortable.

*Start with small jumps and work up to bigger ones.*

*Use your arms and shoulders to help you jump around.*

*Try to turn first one way, then the other.*

**Avoiding injury**
Cold, stiff limbs are prone to injury. You may need to warm up again after a long, cold ride to the mountaintop on an exposed ski lift.

### Jump turns
Jumping up and down on the spot is a good way to get warm. Add a spin of the board, and it's also a useful way to turn around.

## Stretching exercises

Once you are warm from jumping up and down or hiking up a slope carrying your board, you are ready to stretch. Try some of these exercises.

*Try to lift the tail.*

### Final checks
Running through a few exercises will also give you a chance to test the flexibility of an unfamiliar rented board.

### Hot and cold
You will get warm quickly by hiking uphill and riding. But beware, you can cool down equally fast when you stop for a while.

**Even up**
Repeat all of these stretches on each side.

**Move smoothly**
Don't jerk the movements or force your stretches beyond what feels comfortable.

*Let this knee flex slightly.*

*Keep this leg straight.*

**1** Move your weight over the nose of your board. Stretch as far as you can comfortably and hold it for a few seconds. Try to lift the board tail and balance. Then stretch the other way, lifting the nose.

**2** Next, stretch forward and try to reach the toe edge at the nose, then at the tail of the board. Remember to move smoothly. Only reach as far as you can and do not bounce to force the stretch farther.

## Exploring your edges

As a newcomer to the sport, you will find it useful to explore the edges of your board. Your edges are your braking system, so you need to know how to use them. Try rocking back and forth or balancing on them to get used to putting pressure on them.

## Heel edge

Your heel edge is the edge of the board under your heels.

*Use your arms for balance.*

*Straighten your legs and push out your bottom.*

*Put pressure onto the toe edge evenly through both your legs and feet.*

## Toe edge

The toe edge is the edge under your toes. Whenever you are facing uphill, you should be using your toe edge.

*Bend your knees to get onto your toe edge.*

**Breathing**
Try to keep breathing normally through each exercise.

*Keep your arms up.*

*Twist slowly to each side.*

*Make sure you bend sideways, not forward.*

*Stretch up from your waist.*

*Don't worry if you cannot reach your toes.*

*Relax your knees. Don't lock them.*

*Support yourself with one hand on your hip.*

*Keep your legs straight.*

**3** Stretch the backs of your legs by reaching down to your toes, keeping your legs straight. Just stretch and hold. Stand up again slowly so you do not get dizzy.

**4** Now work your upper body. Raise your arms like you are carrying a tray, and rotate as far as you can, twisting from your waist. Hold the position. Repeat on the other side.

**5** Stretch out your sides. Take one arm up over your head and bend sideways; support yourself by placing the opposite hand on your hip. Now you are ready to ride.

# On the move

**A**T FIRST IT WILL feel like your board has a mind of its own. As soon as you start to move, it slides away with you. Learn to "sideslip" and you will be able to keep your board firmly under control, even on the steepest slopes. This is a skill that you can use in any tight spot.

**3** Use your leading hand to help you steer. Keep some pressure on your heel edge to check your speed, and turn your shoulders uphill to slow down.

**2** Place your weight over your front foot and turn your upper body toward the nose. This will start the board moving.

*Face front as your board stops.*

**4** As the board slows to a stop, shift your weight back onto both feet. Come back into a neutral stance with pressure through your heel edge.

**5** Now repeat this process but shift your weight toward the tail, turning your shoulders toward it. This should start you riding "fakie," or backward.

## Diagonal sideslipping

Diagonal sideslipping is like straight sideslipping but you use your weight and rotation at the same time to move diagonally across the slope. Here you can see how to sideslip on your heel edge.

**1** Start in a neutral stance and apply pressure to your heel edge to hold yourself still.

*Keep your hands at waist height.*

*Shift your weight onto this leg and flex your knee.*

*The tail now leads, as you move off riding fakie.*

**6** As you gain confidence, flatten the board slightly from its heel edge and lean more toward the tail to make the board move faster.

# How to sideslip

Sideslipping is a controlled slide downhill keeping your board horizontal across the slope. By alternately digging in an edge to brake and then flattening the board to slide, you can control your descent. You can do this on either the toe edge or the heel edge. Here the technique is shown on the heel edge.

**1** Start in a neutral stance, facing downhill. Dig in your heel edge so the board is still, and keep your weight evenly divided over both feet.

**2** Slowly release the pressure on your heel edge and tilt the board slightly toward the toe edge. As the board flattens, you will start to slide.

**3** To slow down, or stop, tilt the board back onto its heel edge. Keep tilting on and off your heel edge to sideslip slowly downhill.

**Steering to stop**
To steer to a stop, turn your upper body to face more uphill, keeping your weight in the direction of travel.

**Going straight**
On a very gentle slope where there is a flat runout area, you can make a straight glide. In a basic riding stance, let your board run flat, pointing straight downhill. As the ground levels out, you will glide to a standstill.

**Fast or slow**
To go faster, steer the board more steeply down the slope by turning your shoulders and leading hand more downhill. To go slower, do the opposite.

*From this position you can decide whether to continue riding fakie, or switch to riding forward.*

*Turn your shoulders to steer with your leading hand.*

**7** Steer the tail of the board uphill to brake by twisting your upper body and leading arm further around, over the tail.

**8** Put pressure back on through your heel edge. As the board slows, resume your neutral stance, ready to move off again.

*Keep your knees flexed.*

# Toeside traverse and run

TRAVELING DIAGONALLY ACROSS a slope is called traversing. It is a useful skill to learn, since you will use it often during your riding career. Knowing how to traverse will also help overcome any fear of pointing straight downhill as you turn from one edge to the other. As you improve and your confidence increases, point your board farther downhill to run, then bring it back across the slope to slow down. Practicing both toeside and heelside traversing will help you to prepare for the next step, which is turning.

*Use your arms for balance and steering.*

*Lean forward to drive the nose downhill.*

*Put pressure back onto your toe edge.*

*Let your board run flat.*

**3** Rotate your upper body back uphill to slow down and keep control. Let yourself glide to a standstill.

*Keep your legs flexed. They will act as shock absorbers as you travel over bumpy terrain.*

*More pressure on the front foot toe edge will improve grip.*

**2** Sink onto your front foot and steer with your leading hand. Rotate your shoulders downhill.

*Start to turn your shoulders downhill.*

**1** Start on your toe edge. Shift your weight forward and rotate your shoulders to start the board turning slightly downhill.

## Toeside traverse

Practice traversing diagonally across the slope on your toe edge. It is important to have the right amount of body weight over the leading edge of the board. Too much weight and you will accelerate out of control. Striking the right body weight will come with practice.

22

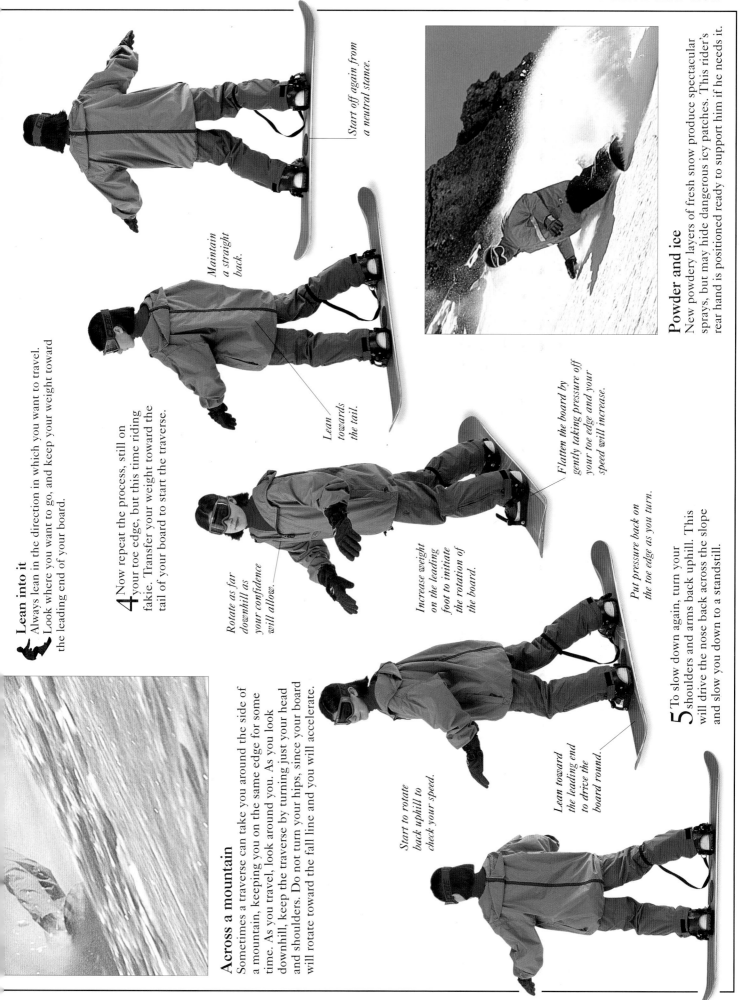

### Powder and ice
New powdery layers of fresh snow produce spectacular sprays, but may hide dangerous icy patches. This rider's rear hand is positioned ready to support him if he needs it.

*Start off again from a neutral stance.*

*Maintain a straight back.*

**Lean into it**
Always lean in the direction in which you want to travel. Look where you want to go, and keep your weight toward the leading end of your board.

4 Now repeat the process, still on your toe edge, but this time riding fakie. Transfer your weight toward the tail of your board to start the traverse.

*Lean towards the tail.*

*Rotate as far downhill as your confidence will allow.*

*Flatten the board by gently taking pressure off your toe edge and your speed will increase.*

*Increase weight on the leading foot to initiate the rotation of the board.*

*Put pressure back on the toe edge as you turn.*

5 To slow down again, turn your shoulders and arms back uphill. This will drive the nose back across the slope and slow you down to a standstill.

*Start to rotate back uphill to check your speed.*

*Lean toward the leading end to drive the board round.*

### Across a mountain
Sometimes a traverse can take you around the side of a mountain, keeping you on the same edge for some time. As you travel, look around you. As you look downhill, keep the traverse by turning just your head and shoulders. Do not turn your hips, since your board will rotate toward the fall line and you will accelerate.

# Heelside traverse and run

THE HEELSIDE EDGE is usually the preferred edge to use when slowing down or stopping during a traverse. You are facing the direction of travel when sideslipping on this edge, and you can therefore gauge more easily how much pressure to apply.

## Heelside traverse

You can start with either heelside or toeside traverses, whichever you find easiest. But you will need to be comfortable on both sides before you can really progress to making turns.

*Look, lean, and point in the direction you are traveling in.*

*Slowly turn your shoulders.*

**1** On your heel edge, bend your front knee, shifting your weight forward. This will start to point the nose downhill.

*Maintain your weight through the leading leg to initiate rotation of the board.*

**2** Steer with your leading hand and bring the nose to point downhill. Allow the board to start running flat.

*As you point downhill, your speed will increase.*

*Take pressure off the heel edge to let the board run.*

**3** Turn your shoulders to take your leading hand back uphill. This will steer the nose back across the slope to slow down.

*Keep your hands lifted.*

*Apply pressure to your heel edge again as you turn.*

## Body weight

Learning how to lean while retaining grip is a skill that will only come with plenty of practice on different surfaces. This rider is leaning far back over his heel edge, but hasn't fallen because he has assessed the surface conditions accurately and knows how to use his body weight to the best advantage.

*Put your body weight over both feet for the most effective heel-edge stop.*

*Steer uphill with your leading hand.*

*Put pressure back on the heel edge.*

*Make all movements smoothly, not suddenly.*

*Look where you are going, not down at your board.*

*Flatten the board and let it run.*

## Edging or running flat

Keep pressure on your working edge except when you want the board to run flat to gain speed. Then return to that edge by putting pressure on it.

**4** Start off across the slope again, but this time riding backward. Begin with your weight on your heel edge and lean toward the tail.

*Tail*

**5** Keep looking in the direction in which you are traveling, and use your leading hand to help you steer.

**6** Check your speed again by rotating your leading arm and shoulders uphill, and run to a standstill, with your board across the slope.

## Surface conditions

You will need to alter your technique according to the type of surface you are on. Here, the snow is very soft, so the rider can afford his body weight to be more over the center of the board. Notice how the arms are open wide to enable the rider to adjust his balance if the surface conditions suddenly change.

# First turns

NOW THAT YOU HAVE started to travel across and down the slope, it is time to start making turns. The secret to turning is learning how to use your weight to put pressure on different parts of the board. The diagram on this page will help you understand where that pressure needs to be applied to make the board turn.

*Keep your leading hand over the edge you are using.*

*Apply pressure through your toe edge.*

*Nose*

*Tail*

**1** Place your board across the slope, with your weight divided equally on both feet, and pressure on your toe edge.

## Heelside turn

The heelside turn starts on the toe edge, glides flat on the base for a moment, and then finishes on the heel edge.

*Flex your knees and keep low.*

**2** Move off slowly by transferring your weight foward onto your front foot and turning your shoulders into a riding stance.

### Pressure points
The shaded areas show where you should be applying pressure to you board to make the turns.

*Rise up slightly to help the board turn.*

**3** As the nose starts to point downhill, extend your arms forward and upward. Release the pressure from your toe edge and let the board flatten.

## Falls
Don't be bothered by falls. Try to remember how to fall safely. Even good riders wipe out occasionally, and sometimes spectacularly!

**4** Start to put pressure on your heel edge through your front foot. Keep your arms high.

**Watch your weight!** Remember, the tail of your board will go too far around and drop downhill if you let your weight shift back on it.

**5** Once the new edge is across the slope, sink onto it and apply pressure to slow you down.

*The next stage will be to link heelside and toeside turns.*

# Toeside turn

The toeside turn starts on your heel edge, turns to run flat through the glide position, and finishes on your toe edge.

*Lean toward the nose of your board.*

*Apply pressure to your heel edge.*

*Tail*

*Start low and flex your knees.*

*Nose*

**1** Start with your board across the slope and use your weight to apply pressure to the heel edge, then move off slowly.

## Practice area

Find a wide-open quiet area on a very gentle slope to practice your first turns. You will find it impossible to keep control on a steep gradient when you start out.

**Slow movements**
Make each movement slowly. Do not rush to change from one pressure point to another.

**2** Lean slightly in the direction you want to go. Shift your weight forward, but keep the pressure on your heel edge.

*Remember to keep looking in the direction you want to go.*

*Make sure your leading hand always stays over the edge you are using.*

*Keep your arms high until the board has come all the way around.*

**3** As the board turns downhill, straighten your legs as if to rise off the board; move your arms up and forward.

**4** Sink back into your board by flexing your knees and direct pressure forward through the toe edge. Let the tail drift around.

**5** Keep the pressure going through the toe edge to bring the board slowly back across the slope.

*Keep your brakes active by flexing your knees.*

**Leading hands**
Note that your leading hand moves to stay over the edge you are using throughout each turn.

# Linking turns

NOW THE FUN can really start. Once you have mastered basic turns on both toeside and heelside, you are ready to start linking them together. This means you will be able to make your way smoothly down a slope without stopping. Be sure to get things right on a gentle slope before you move on to a steeper one.

## Basic linked turns

Find an easy slope with plenty of space and start by trying to link just two or three turns together at a time.

*Start to turn your shoulders and hips downhill.*

*Straighten your legs to help the board come around.*

*Let the board run flat.*

*Keep your hands forward.*

*Look where you want to go.*

*Keep your weight on your toe edge.*

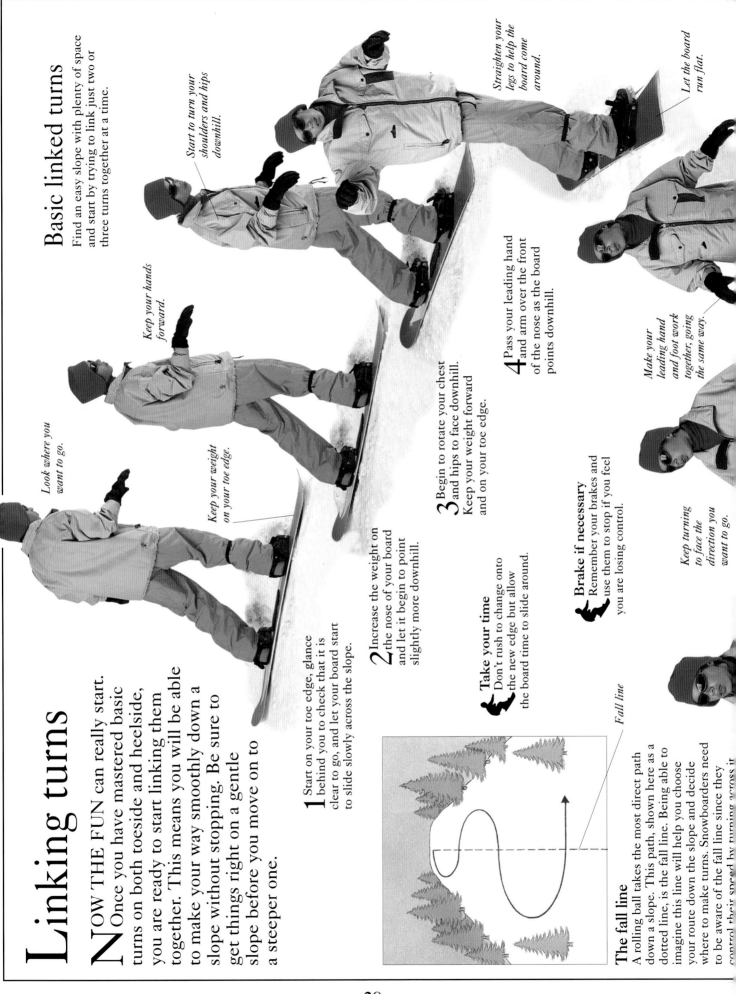

*Make your leading hand and foot work together, going the same way.*

*Keep turning to face the direction you want to go.*

**1** Start on your toe edge, glance behind you to check that it is clear to go, and let your board start to slide slowly across the slope.

**2** Increase the weight on the nose of your board and let it begin to point slightly more downhill.

**3** Begin to rotate your chest and hips to face downhill. Keep your weight forward and on your toe edge.

**4** Pass your leading hand and arm over the front of the nose as the board points downhill.

**Take your time** Don't rush to change onto the new edge but allow the board time to slide around.

**Brake if necessary** Remember your brakes and use them to stop if you feel you are losing control.

*Fall line*

## The fall line

A rolling ball takes the most direct path down a slope. This path, shown here as a dotted line, is the fall line. Being able to imagine this line will help you choose your route down the slope and decide where to make turns. Snowboarders need to be aware of the fall line since they control their speed by turning across it.

**5** Keep your weight forward and start to go onto your heel edge. Keep the turn going by driving the board with your legs.

### Extending
Straightening your legs makes you lift up. This takes your weight off the board, making it easier to turn.

### Flexing
Flexing your knees makes you use your weight to steer and control the board.

*Start to put weight on your heel edge.*

**6** Bend your knees and sink into your board. This will make your heel edge work and help you control your speed.

*Flex your knees and feel the new edge start to grip under your front foot.*

**7** Lean forward and start to prepare your arms to pass back over the nose again as you make the next turn.

### Knowing your limits
Once you can control your turns, steer, and stop, you can really start to enjoy mountains. But know the limit of your skills and stick to marked runs appropriate for your level of experience. Don't be tempted to try the difficult runs yet, or go off the marked routes.

*Bend your knees and shift your weight forward.*

*Sink down to increase pressure on your toe edge.*

*Keep your back straight. Don't slouch.*

**8** Stay high and forward on your board until you turn onto the new edge.

*Let the tail follow around freely.*

**9** Flex your knees and sink down on your toe edge again to bring your speed under control.

# Carving turns

**P**ROGRESSING TO CARVED turns will really open up snowboarding for you. Carving means using the edge of the board to cut a track in the snow as you turn. The change of edge takes place earlier than on basic turns and the tail no longer slides around, slowing you down, but follows the track of the nose.

**1** Start with a fairly steep toeside traverse. This will allow you to build up the speed you need to carve your turns.

*Push your weight forward.*

## The heelside carve

The heelside carve starts on the toe edge but you change to the heel edge before the board crosses the fall line. The curve of the board edge makes the board turn, carving its way around.

*Start to rotate your shoulders and leading arm.*

*Keep your back straight.*

**2** Apply pressure to your heel edge as you turn your head, shoulders, leading arm, and hip in the direction of the turn.

**3** Sink your body weight into the heel edge by pushing your hips over it. This will make the edge grip.

*Change onto your heel edge.*

*Tuck your rear knee in toward your front leg.*

**Fluid motion**
As you improve, try to change from edge to edge in a fluid, easy motion.

*Sink over the heel edge.*

*Keep your arms wide for stability.*

**4** As soon as the turn is complete, start to extend your legs. Push up from your heel edge, letting the board run flat, and prepare to link into the next toeside turn.

**Making it flow**
Link the rotation of your upper body with the up-and-down motion of your legs and your turns will start to flow.

# The toeside carve

The toeside carve is like the heelside turn, but it starts on the heel edge. Carving turns means linking toeside and heelside turns, one after the other, to carve your way smoothly and rhythmically down a slope, leaving an S-shaped track.

**1** Prepare for the turn with a heelside traverse across the slope. You need to be moving to carve successfully.

*Build up speed on a steep heelside traverse.*

*Start to rotate your shoulders.*

*Hold your arms out to help you balance.*

*Keep your weight forward in the traverse position.*

**2** As you gather speed, rotate your shoulders and arms in the direction of the turn. Roll the board onto your toe edge.

*Roll onto your toe edge.*

**3** Bring your leading arm around and flex your knees to sink your body weight into your toe edge.

*Keep your back straight. Don't bend at the waist.*

*The amount you lean depends on the speed you are going.*

*Look and lean into the turn.*

*Flex your knees and ankles.*

**4** Once the board crosses the fall line and has carved around, start to extend and prepare for the next heelside turn.

*The edge change takes place before the board crosses the fall line.*

**Extreme lean**
By going faster and edging the board correctly, you will find yourself leaning more into your turns, as shown here.

# Ground tricks

## Tail slide

The tail slide is the first stage of many tricks and spins. Once you can do a basic slide there are lots of variations to try. As you practice, experiment with how and where to place your weight. Use your rear arm to help distribute your weight along the board.

FREESTYLE RIDING is all about tricks and spins on the ground and in the air. The tricks are as varied as your imagination, and fun to try, but you will need to master your basic skills first. Learning to do nose and tail slides, spin, and ride fakie are all important skills that form the basis for many more advanced and aerial tricks.

*Keep your head up.*

*Keep your back straight.*

**1** Start with a straight run in a relaxed riding stance with the board running flat.

*Keep the pressure on through your back foot.*

*Keep the whole of the board base flat.*

**2** Shift your weight onto your rear foot and spread your arms out for balance.

### Crouching low

Crouch as low as possible when jumping and on landing. Crouching gives more spring to your jump and therefore more height. As you land, flex your legs to cushion your landing.

**Keep it up**
Try to keep the nose in the air longer each time you practice the tail slide.

### Riding fakie

This regular rider has his leading foot facing up the hill. This is called riding fakie. The basic rules still apply for riding fakie down a hill. Place weight on your downhill leg, and look and point in the direction of travel. With practice, you will be able to ride backward with the same degree of skill as riding forward. To return to riding forward, you can either come to a stop and start off in the opposite direction, spin around on the nose or tail, or jump around 180 degrees.

*Use your arms to help you balance.*

**5** Take your weight forward again to bring the nose down.

*Flex your front leg when landing to soak up the shock.*

*Keep your front leg straight during the jump.*

**3** Use your front leg to pull up the nose and keep your arms stretched out.

**4** Keep your weight on your back foot and hold the nose in the air.

# Ground spins

SPINS AND OTHER GROUND TRICKS are sometimes referred to as "old school," since they are closely related to moves used in skateboarding and surfing. However, these tricks will give you invaluable grounding in the basic skills necessary for performing successful aerial tricks and will also give you a good understanding of how your board works.

*Keep your stance relaxed as you start to prepare for this trick.*

*Your shoulders should remain facing forward.*

*Crouch low for more spring on takeoff.*

*Take your arms back ready to help you turn.*

*Start to sink down on to your front foot.*

*Use rotation of the upper body to bring the board around during a spin.*

*Nose*

*Lift the tail by straightening your back leg.*

**1** From a straight run, bring all your weight onto your front leg and bend your front knee slightly.

*Flex your front knee.*

*As you spin, don't let the board edge catch the surface.*

## Nose slide to fakie

As you gain in skill and confidence, you may feel ready to experiment with some new moves. This nose slide includes a 180-degree spin and finishes riding fakie.

**2** Keep your shoulders facing forward, but take your arms back behind you and lift the tail of the board.

### Fakie nose slide

Like a cyclist doing a wheelie, this rider can probably hold this slide for some time, as long as he keeps just the right amount of pressure over the nose. Too much or too little and the board will simply slip away from under him. This ground trick can be used as part of a routine, like a 360-degree nose spin.

**Before and after**
Takeoffs and landings should be done with the board facing the direction of travel. The board should be as flat and free running as possible.

**Rotation**
Rotate your hips as you turn your shoulders and the board will spin around.

## In a spin
Once you have accomplished getting your board off the ground, you will want to try to spin it. Notice how this rider is bringing the nose of the board around by rotating his upper body. His head and shoulders rotate first and the hips and legs are free to follow. To keep the board high enough above the ground for spinning, you may need to tuck your legs up so that the edges of the board do not catch the surface.

*Use your arms to help you turn.*

*Avoid landing on the board edge with the board across the fall line as this will instantly cause the board to lose momentum.*

*Keep your body weight over the board during tricks to avoid landing body first.*

*You are now riding fakie but still traveling in the same direction.*

**3** Keep the tail up in the air. Then rotate your arms and upper body forward using the movement to spin the tail of the board around.

**4** Keep the board moving until the tail has come around 180 degrees, driving it on with your back leg.

**5** Your rear leg is now leading as you put the tail down on the ground. Shift your weight onto it – you are now riding fakie.

# Tricks in the air

TRICKS IN THE AIR are not just for the most daring or talented riders. Once you have mastered good basic riding techniques you will be surprised how easy some exciting-looking tricks can be. Start by practicing "ollie" (small jump using your own energy to take off) and jumps from small hits, or bumps, on the slope and gradually build up your confidence. Make sure you are aware of other slope users at all times.

### Finding air
Jumps, or airs, can be turned into all kinds of exciting tricks if you have the skill and imagination. Here you can see a heel edge grab. There are endless ways to grab your board – on either edge, by the nose or tail, or with either hand. Further variations, all with different names, can be made by "boning out," or straightening, one or the other of your legs.

## A fakie backside 180-degree indy
You will need to build up confidence and progress from straight jumps and practice spins and grabs before tackling this trick. It starts from a fakie (riding backward so tail of the board leads) takeoff and includes a spin of 180 degrees with a grab on the toeside edge.

**Safe jumping**
Check that you have a clear run up to the jump and that there is a big, safe landing area, clear of rocks and people.

*Take your trailing arm high to help you balance.*

**3** As you take off, use the forward rotation of your shoulders and arms, like a spring uncoiling, to start your spin.

*Rotate your arms and shoulders, in the opposite direction of your spin.*

**4** Keep your board level by spreading your weight equally. Reach down with your front arm and grab the toe edge.

*Lift the tail slightly on takeoff. Don't let it drop.*

*Grab the toe edge between your feet.*

**1** Move off smoothly, riding in a confident fakie stance. Keep your head up and look forward. Try not to look at the drop.

**2** As you approach the jump, start to prepare. Flex back onto your rear leg and start to rotate your shoulders, pulling your arms back.

# Ollies

You can use ollies to go over small obstacles for fun. Practice springing up and down on the spot, taking off front foot first. Then try it on the move, starting from a basic riding posture.

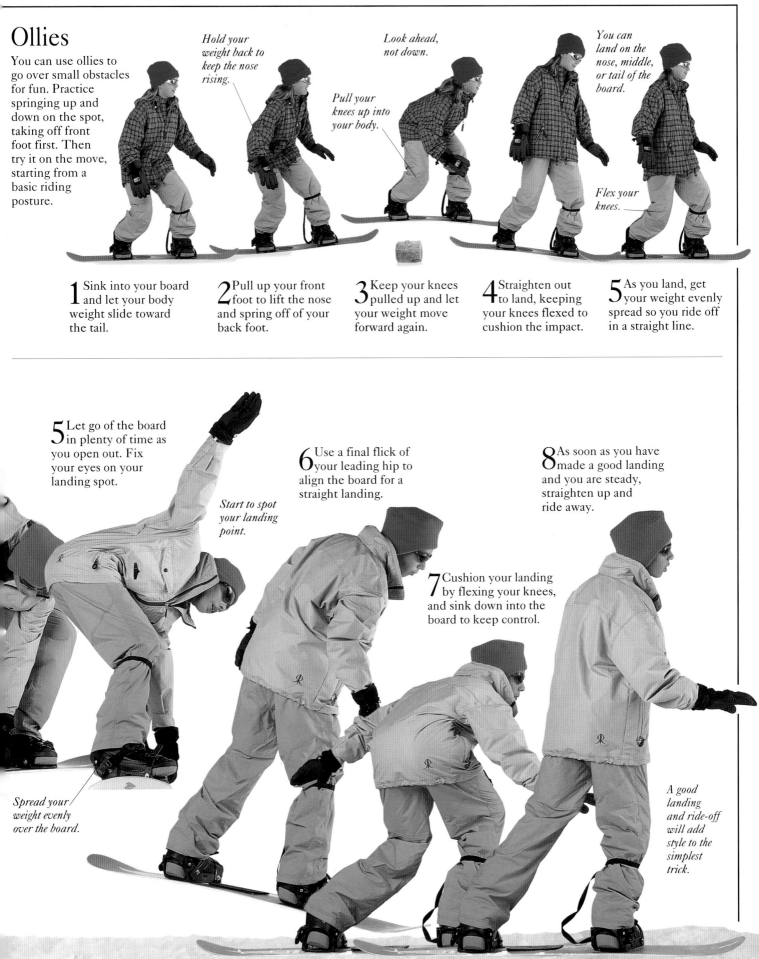

*Hold your weight back to keep the nose rising.*

*Look ahead, not down.*

*Pull your knees up into your body.*

*You can land on the nose, middle, or tail of the board.*

*Flex your knees.*

**1** Sink into your board and let your body weight slide toward the tail.

**2** Pull up your front foot to lift the nose and spring off of your back foot.

**3** Keep your knees pulled up and let your weight move forward again.

**4** Straighten out to land, keeping your knees flexed to cushion the impact.

**5** As you land, get your weight evenly spread so you ride off in a straight line.

**5** Let go of the board in plenty of time as you open out. Fix your eyes on your landing spot.

*Start to spot your landing point.*

**6** Use a final flick of your leading hip to align the board for a straight landing.

**8** As soon as you have made a good landing and you are steady, straighten up and ride away.

**7** Cushion your landing by flexing your knees, and sink down into the board to keep control.

*Spread your weight evenly over the board.*

*A good landing and ride-off will add style to the simplest trick.*

# Slalom racing

**R**ACING THROUGH THE gates of a slalom course set on a zigzag downhill path is a very exciting riding style and differs from freestyle or freeriding – slalom is all about speed and accuracy in a series of left and right turns. Racers use long, specially prepared boards and hard boots to gain the extra speed and fine-tuned control needed for top-level competitions. Competitions are arranged for every level and you may find it fun to take part.

## Slalom technique

For this type of riding, use the edges of your board not as brakes, but to direct the board. The less you slow down, the better. Your upper body should sweep and rotate over the nose of the board in a steady rhythm, synchronized with a pumping action from your legs. The speed of racing means that you should always wear a safety helmet.

*Wear a helmet for safety.*

*Flex your knees to stay low.*

*Using race wax on the base makes the board run faster.*

*Allow the board to flatten.*

*Use your arms for balance.*

**1** Start to line up with the gate ahead. Stay low on your board and keep pressure on the toe edge.

**Boot fitting**
Make sure your boots fit really well so that all your movements transfer precisely to the board.

**2** Extend your legs slightly to start the edge change. Let the board flatten and accelerate momentarily.

**3** Sink into your heel edge, flexing your knees to get low. Widen your arms to keep your balance.

*Start to look for the next gate.*

**4** Hold your heel edge as the nose of the board passes the gate and focus on the next gate.

*Slalom gate*

**Top-level competition**
In competition, every fraction of a second counts. Race boards are carefully prepared with special waxes and edged for maximum speed and cut. The racers wear skintight suits to cut down on air resistance and protective equipment such as helmets and arm and leg guards to help prevent injury.

**5** Rise up from the heel edge gradually to release the brakes and increase speed.

*Let your board flatten again.*

**6** Run flat toward the next gate and plan the line and timing for your next turn.

**Leg protection**
A protective guard on the leading leg reduces the chance of injury if a racer hits one of the gates.

**Racing events**
There are several different slalom events, such as giant slalom and super G. They vary in the length and width of the course but are all raced against the clock. Boardercross, shown here, is a fairly new event. It is a group race and includes all aspects of snowboarding – from slalom to freeriding and freestyle.

**7** Shift your weight onto the tail to lift the nose and help you make a quicker edge change.

*Drive yourself on to the finish line.*

**Arm protection**
Cutting as close to the gates as possible, many racers push the flexible posts out of their way. They wear arm guards for safety.

**8** Sink into your toe edge, shifting your weight forward to the nose. This will control your turn, making it carve through the gate.

*Get low on your toe edge.*

39

# Other snowboarding events

SNOWBOARDING is a popular and rapidly growing sport. Events are held at every level, from local events at dry slopes, through to national and worldwide championships on snow. Top results in these competitions can turn you into a household name! Whether you dream of representing your country at an Olympic event one day or just enjoy the thrill and freedom of snowboarding, it is a sport that will guarantee hours of excitement.

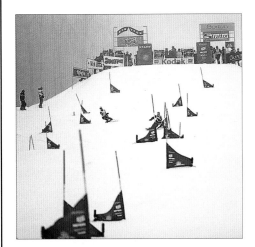

### Dual slalom
A slalom race, through gates, is against the clock, with the fastest rider winning. In dual slalom, two riders race against each other, and the clock, on parallel courses.

### Half pipe
A half pipe is a U-shaped channel dug into snow. Freestylers ride up the steep sides of the pipe to pull off amazing aerial tricks. Points are given for style, height, and difficulty of the tricks shown.

### Olympic gold
Snowboarding first featured in the 1998 Winter Olympics, held in Nagano, Japan. Canadian Ross Rebagliati, shown here, won the gold medal in the giant slalom event.

## Boardercross

This is a very exciting event for both spectators and participants, since it includes riders who normally race and carve and freestylers who are more at home pulling big air tricks. They race in heats of six competitors. Slalom-style gates set the course through banked turns called burns. The course usually involves big humps and hits to negotiate, too.

## Dryslope competition

Dryslopes are used where access to snow is limited. In competition, freestylers use ramps to take off and the judging of their tricks is similar to that of halfpipe events.

## Big air

Big air is one of the most spectacular and acrobatic of all snowboarding events. Competitors launch into the air from a ramp and perform amazing spins, inverts, and other aerial tricks.

## Freeriding

Many snowboard enthusiasts feel the excitement of snowboarding lies, not in competition, but in being out and about in the mountains. Making flawless tracks in fresh snow, or finding natural jumps and gullies to ride, offers challenge enough without the formalities of organized events and competitions. This makes freeriding the most popular event of them all!

# Glossary

When learning to snowboard, or watching boarding events, you may find it helpful to understand the meaning of some of the following words and terms.

**180** A spin of 180°, or half a circle.
**360** A 360° spin, also known as a "3," where the rider rotates full circle.
**540** A spin of 540°, or one and a half circles, also known as a "5."

## A

**Aerial** A maneuver or trick that is performed in midair.
**Air** A jump or leap from the ground, usually taking off from a ramp or hit.
**Air-to-fakie** A halfpipe trick where the rider approaches the wall forward, lands, then returns back down the wall without turning around.
**Arm guards** Worn by slalom racers to protect their arms and hands when cutting close to the gates.

## B

**Backside** A term to describe a trick in which the rotation brings the heel edge around first.
**Bail** A term for the metal clips used in the hard-boot system. They are part of the bindings on the board and secure the heel and toe of your boot in position. The step-in system uses metal bails that are attached to the sole of the boot.
**Base** The bottom surface of a snowboard.
**Big air** A term that is used to describe a particularly high jump. A launch ramp and landing area allows a rider to stay higher for longer in the air.
**Bindings** Devices that attach your boots to the board. They are always non-release.
**Boardercross** A racing event for six racers, on a course including slalom-style gates, banked turns, and humps.
**Boning out** Straightening one or both your legs during a jump.

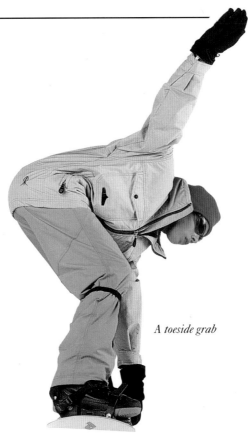

*A toeside grab*

**BSA** The British Snowboard Association; the sole British representative and sanctioning body of the ISF.

## C

**Camber** The raised middle part of the board.
**Carve** The way an experienced rider uses the shaped edges of the board to make smooth turns that cut into the surface.
**Catching air** A term to describe the time you are in the air during a trick or jump.

## D

**Dryslope** An artificial slope covered in plastic bristles to create a surface on which people can snowboard or ski.
**Dual slalom** A slalom race event in which competitors race two at a time on parallel courses.

## E

**Edging** Applying pressure to the working edge of your board.
**Effective edge** The board edges that touch the snow.
**Eurocarve** The way a rider inclines or banks into a hill or edge so much that his or her arm and body touch the snow.

*Performing a jump.*

**Extend** The action of straightening your legs to lift your body weight up from the board.

## F

**Fakie** Riding backward so that the tail of the board leads.
**Fall line** An imaginary line that would form the most direct, and therefore steepest, path down a slope.
**Flex** A term to describe bending the knees and ankles to control the board or absorb the impact of bumps and ridges on the slope. Also a term used to describe the flexibility of the board itself.
**Freeriding** The informal and noncompetitive style of snowboarding for fun, making the most of the natural mountain terrain. This is the most common type of snowboarding.
**Freestyle** A style of snowboarding that incorporates tricks, jumps, and halfpipe riding, emphasising style rather than speed.
**Frontside** A term to describe a trick in which the rotation brings the toe edge round first.

## G

**Garland** Continuous swings to the hill from the fall line on one edge only.
**Gates** The colored posts and panels on a slalom course that mark the route for competitors to follow.

*Hard boot with ratcheted fastenings*

**Giant slalom (GS)** A slalom race event on a course at least 60 ft (20 m) wide and with a vertical drop between 395 and 985 ft (120 and 300 m).
**Goofy** A term to describe a rider's stance in which the right foot is in the front binding.
**Grab** To take hold of the snowboard with one or both hands during a jump.
**Gradient** The steepness of the slope.

## H

**Halfpipe** A U-shaped channel dug into snow for freestyle riding and competition.
**Handplant** A halfpipe trick when a rider inverts at the top of the halfpipe, and holds onto the lip, or coping with one or both hands.

*Landing after a jump.*

**Hard boots** Rigid boots with a plastic outer shell, usually preferred by racers. The stiffness of the boots helps the rider to transfer body movements to the board.
**Heel edge** The edge of the board under your heels, regardless of goofy or regular stance.
**Hit** A bump in the snow, or a jump, from which riders launch themselves.

**I**
**Indy** A trick jump in which a grab is made between the feet on the toe edge, with the back hand.
**Inserts** Small threaded holes in the board that enable you to mount the bindings in different places.
**International Snowboard Federation (ISF)** The world-wide governing body of snowboarding.
**Invert** An aerial trick in which the rider is upside down.

**L**
**Leash** A safety strap, which links the board to the rider to stop it sliding away and being a danger to other slope users.

**M**
**Method air** An aerial trick in which you kick the board up behind you, and use your front hand to grab the heelside edge.
**Moguls** A series of offset bumps.

**N**
**Nollie** Similar to an Ollie, but the rider springs off of the nose.

**Nose** The front end of the snowboard.
**Nose slide** A ground trick, lifting the tail of the board and sliding on the nose.

**O**
**Ollie** A small jump in which the rider springs into the air off of the tail, using his or her own energy to leave the ground.

**P**
**Park** An area set aside for snowboarding.
**Pumping** An up-and-down action of the rider's legs to build up momentum and/or height.

**R**
**Ramp** A natural, or artificial, slope from which riders can launch into the air.
**Ratcheted fastenings** A type of fastening found on hard boots and also on soft bindings.
**Regular** A term to describe a rider's stance in which the left foot is in the front binding.

**S**
**Scoot** Pushing with your free foot to make the board glide forward.
**Sideslip** A method of sliding down the slope with the board at 90 degrees to the fall line, and using the uphill edge to control the descent.
**Slalom** A race event through the gates of a marked course.
**Soft boots** Flexible lace-up snowboarding boots used by most freestylers and many freeriders.
**Stance** The position in which you stand on the board.
**Step-in boots and bindings** An integrated system of boots with metal bails that clip into spring-loaded, non-release bindings.
**Stomp pad** A nonslip pad next to the rear binding, where you can rest your free foot when scooting.
**Straight running** Keeping the board flat.
**Super G** A slalom race event on a course at least 98 ft (30 m) wide and with a vertical drop of between 985 and 1,640 ft (300 and 500 m).

*Regular*          *Goofy*

**T**
**Tail** The back end of the board.
**Tail slide** A ground trick, where you lift the nose of the board and slide along on the tail.
**Toe edge** The edge under your toes, regardless of your stance.
**Traversing** Moving diagonally across a slope.

**V**
**Vert** The vertical part of a halfpipe wall.

**W**
**Waist** The narrowest part of a snowboard between the nose and tail.
**Warm up** Essential preparation before every riding session to warm and stretch muscles and joints and help prevent injury.
**Wax** A preparation applied to the base of a snowboard to help it run smoothly.
**Wipe out** A spectacular fall.

*Standing up after a fall.*

# Index

# Useful addresses

Here are the addresses of some snowboarding organizations, which you may find useful.

**United States Amateur Snowboard Association (USASA)**
P.O. Box 756
Truckee, CA 96160
Tel: (800) 404-9213
Fax: (530) 582-4672
Website: www.usasa.org

**United States Snowboarding Association (USSA)**
P.O. Box 100
1500 Kearns Blvd
Park City, UT 84060
Tel: (435) 649-9090
Fax: (435) 649-3613
Website: www.usskiteam.com

**American Pro Snowboard**
2525 Ocean Park Blvd.
2nd floor,
Santa Monica, CA 90405
Tel: (310) 452-3599
Fax: (310) 452-3889

**Canadian Ski Council**
2800 Skymark Ave, Suite 32
Mississauga,
Ontario, L4W 5A6
Canada
Tel: (905) 212-9040
Website: www.skicanada.org
Email: info@skicanada.org

**Canadian Association of Snowboard Instructors**
774 boul. Décaire, Suite 310
Ville St. Laurent,
Québec, H4L 5H7
Canada
Tel: 1 (800) 811-6428
Website: www.snopro.com
Email: alliance@snopro.com

Rachel    Arash    Kate    Tariq    Ryan

## Acknowledgments

Dorling Kindersley would like to thank the following people
for their help in the production of this book:

All the young snowboarders for their patience and enthusiasm during the photographic sessions; 1-2-Freeride, Radair, Nice, and Burton for the equipment loaned; Nicholas Hewetson for diagrammatic illustrations; Patricia Grogan for additional editorial assistance; Joanna Malivoire for additional design assistance; Sally Hamilton for picture research; Giles Powell-Smith for the jacket design.

The publisher would like to thank the following for their kind permission to reproduce their photographs:

a=above; c=center; b=below; l=left; r=right; t=top

**Picture Credits**
**Action Plus:** DPPI 23tr; Neil Tingle 35tr; P. Millereau/DPPI 40tr; Peter Blakeman 22/23b.

**Allsport:** 19cl; Anton Want 11cr; Mike Cooper 38br; Mike Hewitt 41bl; Shaun Botterill 40b. **AppalSport:** Sang Tan 11bl, 11bc, 39tr. **Burton Snowboards:** 10tl, 11tl, 29cr, 31bl. **Lee Irvine:** 41cl. **Jonno Gibbins:** 27tr. **John Layshock:** 10cl, 10bl, 10br, back jacket cr. **Sang Tan:** 24/25, 32bl, 33tr, 34bl, 40cl, 41br. **Sims Sports:** 11c. **Skishoot Offshoot:** Adrian Myers 25br. **Stockshot:** Gary Pearl 41tr; Jess Stock Endpapers, 26bl, 36tr.

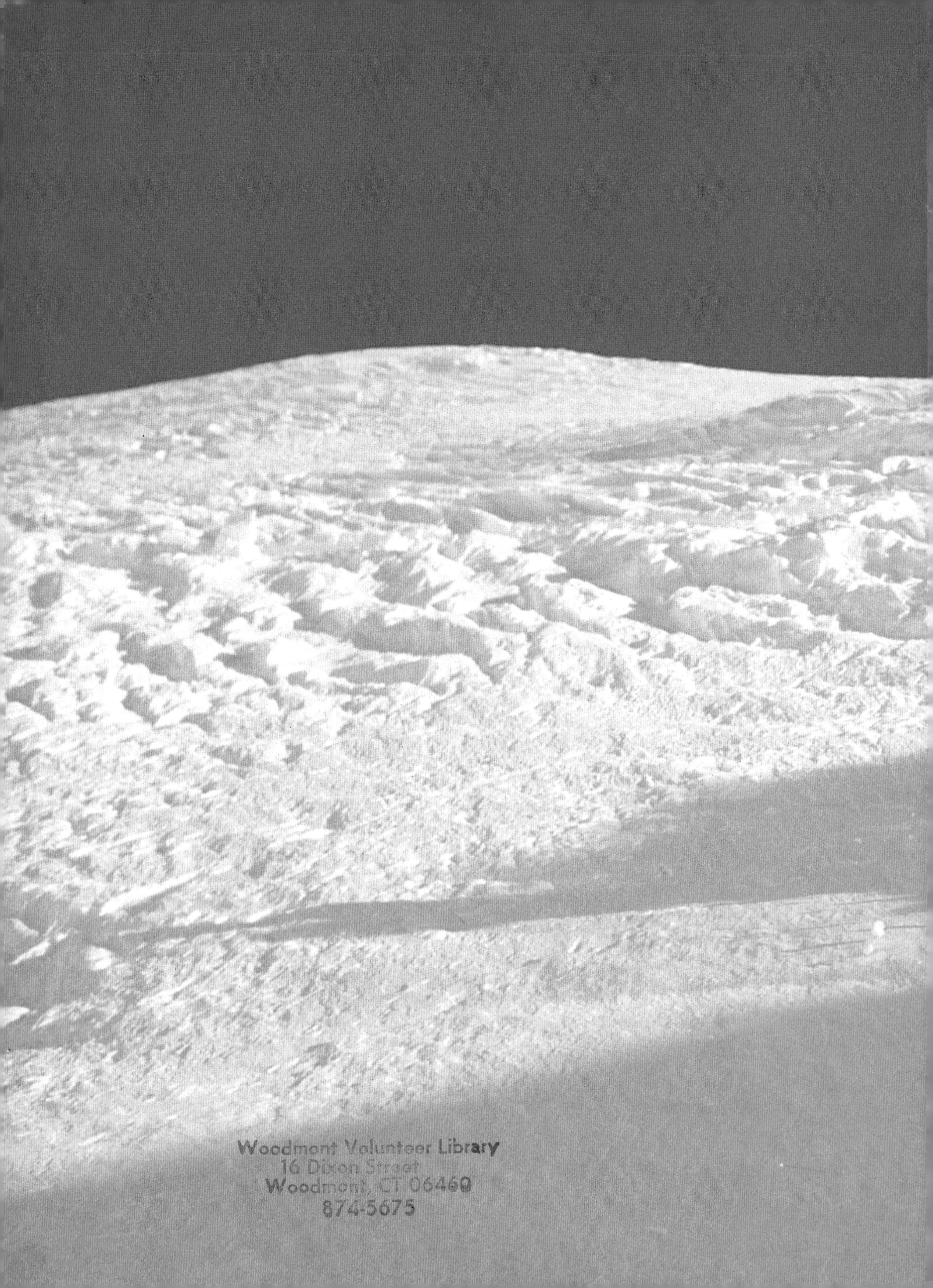